WICCA HERBAL MAGIC

A Solitary Practitioner's Guide to Using Herbs and Plants in Wiccan Rituals. A Crash Course to Herbal Spells, Herbal Magic, Candle Magic, and Moon Magic (2022 for Beginners)

Tess Robinson

TABLE OF CONTENTS

INTRODUCTION

We congratulate you on your purchase of the book Wicca Herbal Magic and appreciate your investment.

Recognizing the power of plants and what they are capable of in terms of herbal magic is a rare awakening. When you decide to explore the world of herbs, you can truly enhance your life in a variety of ways.

This book will provide you with a wealth of information. It discusses the history of herbalism and how to get started with herbs. You will gain invaluable knowledge about purchasing, growing, caring for, and storing some of the most widely used magical herbs.

Additionally, information on herbal baths, teas, sachets, and essential oils will be included. Each of these components contributes to your ability to fulfil your life's desires and needs. Herbal teas can also assist you in your magical practises, and we will discuss several excellent teas for divination, energy, good fortune, and prosperity.

Without spells, no Wicca herbal magic book would be complete. You'll have access to a variety of beginner-friendly spells.

There are spells for success, wealth, fortune, love, and health, among others!

Not only will you gain access to spells, but you'll also learn about various types of magical boosters that you can incorporate into your herbal spells. Candles, crystals, stones, gems, and meditation will all be discussed. Enhancing the effectiveness of your spells does not have to be difficult.

Herbal remedies have been shown to be more beneficial than pharmaceutical medications. Naturally, many people prefer to go natural.

You can heal yourself using the enchanted properties of herbs. They can aid in the treatment of inflammation, infection, and immune function, among other things.

Finally, you'll receive a guide to full-moon magic. The moon possesses an incredible amount of power, which can be advantageously harnessed. With the moon's power, you can forecast outcomes and plan your life.

There are numerous books on this subject available; once again, thank you for selecting this one! Every effort has been made to ensure that it is as comprehensive as possible; please enjoy!

CHAPTER 1:

INTRODUCTION TO HERBALISM

Chapter one will provide background information on herbalism, ensuring that you have a firm foundation of knowledge. It will cover the history of herbalism and some of the most prominent figures in the field. Additionally, you will discover why herbs are so significant in magical practises.

Shamanism is also a component of herbal magic and is a component of Wiccan beliefs. We'll swoon over any information you provide on this subject.

Finally, this chapter will teach you how to improve your communication with plant spirits. This can lead you to more powerful spells that manifest more easily than those you've attempted previously.

Having a positive relationship with nature will have a beneficial effect on your spell casting practises.

To comprehend herbalism, we must first examine what it is. When people discuss herbalism, they are referring to the use of plants or plant extracts in folk and traditional medicine. An herbalist is someone who has become knowledgeable about plants and their medicinal properties. It takes time to acquire the knowledge, but once acquired, it opens up a world of possibilities for living a healthier, more natural lifestyle.

Herbalism, like everything else, has evolved significantly over time. What we see today is not what we saw in the past; however, there will always be parallels. So how did herbalism get to where it is today?

Herbal medicine has been practised on a global scale for, well, practically ever. It's difficult to pinpoint exactly when it all began, as it has always existed. There is evidence that Paleolithic people practised herbalism. As you can see, that was an aeon ago. Herbalism runs deep in our ancestors. It is critical to remember that herbs used during this time period may have been viewed as food rather than for their medicinal and magical properties.

As time passed, the use of herbs gained popularity.

Around 30,000 BCE, the Shamans practised herbalism for the first time. Within a variety of different tribes, shamans are the keepers of healing and medicine. Shamans were renowned for their ability to communicate with the earth and the spirits of plants. They were said to be able to communicate with superior beings. These higher powers would assist them in determining the best method for healing their people. This was frequently accomplished through the use of herbal remedies and medicines.

Shamans documented their herbal practises through cave drawings.

Herbalism's first documented history occurred on clay tablets. They were etched into them by Mesopotamia's Sumerians. Simultaneously, Chinese medicine was being documented, and it included a plethora of herbs and plants. These teachings were also passed down verbally between a herbalist teacher and their student in India.

Around the same time period, the Egyptians began compiling written records on the medicinal properties of herbs and plants.

They compiled a number of different medical texts that assisted in the description of herbs, their properties, and their applications. Several of the pieces of information they provided are still highly regarded today.

Herbs continued to play a significant role in medicine and healing over time. Whether from a Christian or a Pagan perspective, the power of herbs cannot be denied. There were times when herbalism was regarded as witchcraft and shunned; however, it never truly died out. For generations, people have consistently practised herbalism, and this will never change.

Herbs have always been important in magic. Let us not forget that plants have existed on this planet much longer than humans have. This is why many people understand why herbs and plants are such valuable additions to your magical toolkit.

Herbal properties are well-known for their ability to aid in physical and spiritual healing. There are numerous plants, and each one possesses unique properties that can be incorporated into magical workings. There was a time when medicine and magic were inextricably linked. It was not just about the herbs; it was also about the rituals and mantras used to confirm that someone was truly on the path of healing.

There is a distinction between medicine and magic in today's world; however, this is not true for everyone. Many can immediately see how they interact to create powerful effects. When magical herbs are combined with spells, rituals, and incantations, astounding results occur. That is why herbs will always be a significant component of magical endeavours.

Herbs & Mysticism

Due to their association with the elements, herbs and plants also play a role in Wiccan practises. Herbs and plants are made up of four primary elements. They originate in the earth, are nourished by the sun and rain, and provide us with oxygen.

They interact with the elements in a variety of ways; however, this illustrates the relationship between plants and the elements. Each and every plant contains all four of the major elements with which we come into contact.

From ancient times to the present, there has been a belief that plants possess a soul or spirit. Philosophers, Wiccans, and witches all concur on the veracity of this statement. Surprisingly, a sizable number of scientists believe in the consciousness of plants as well.

This consciousness enables plants to communicate with one another and with us. There is evidence that plants will cooperate to aid their neighbouring foliage. They accomplish this through their root systems.

Nutrients can be exchanged between plants. If one plant, tree, or shrub is deficient in a particular area, others will assist it in surviving.

Interestingly, they can also assist one another in avoiding predators. A good example of this is insects that consume leaves.

When a bug begins chomping on a leaf, plants release chemicals to alert other plants to follow suit. This chemical release serves two purposes. Along with alerting other plants to the presence of a predator, it also helps repel the insect from the plant on which it is currently feeding.

All of these factors contribute to demonstrating how intelligent plants are and the type of power they possess. Witches and Wiccans will use this power to energise their spellcasting and aid in the manifestation of a variety of different desires, wants, and needs. It makes no difference which part of the plant you are working with; it may hold the key to spellcasting success.

Plants and herbs are incredibly versatile when it comes to magic. They are inextricably linked to the earth and can provide you with its energy. It is preferable to grow and use your herbs because you can charge them with the necessary energy as you cultivate and grow them. Growing them gives you direct access to the energies of all four of the primary elements: earth, air, fire, and water.

Herbs are incorporated into a plethora of different spells. You can use them to make spell jars, poppets, pillows, sachets, and a variety of other charms. Additionally, they are frequently used to create essential oils and incense. This can provide you with increased magical energy and the ability to cast more powerful spells.

Herbs are frequently used in witchcraft. From candle or crystal spells to purification and blessings, herbs can assist in achieving long-lasting results. Herbs are incorporated into a variety of cultures and traditions. This is because they are extremely powerful, and their utility has been demonstrated time and time again.

There is an abundance of information available regarding herbs and their use in magical practises. At first, it may appear intimidating.

Recognize that it will become easier with time, study, and dedication. Later in this book, we'll discuss some of the essential herbs for performing spells, rituals, incantations, and other magical operations. You will gain a solid foundation of knowledge that will enable you to begin working with herbs immediately.

Herbalism's Pioneers

While herbalism has a long history, there are a few individuals who helped pave the way for its popularity and practical application. In reality, a large number of people contributed; however, some were more significant than others. Understanding the pioneers of herbalism will help you develop a firm understanding of why herbalism is still so vital and widely used today.

Hippocrates is one of the first names that should be mentioned when discussing herbalism pioneers. His well-known quote, "Let your food be your medicine and your medicine be your food," is extremely well-known and provides us with some of the earliest insights into the healing properties of herbs and plants. He educated the public about the vital role herbs play in our survival and health.

Hippocrates was not a particularly spiritual person. He was far more rational. He used herbal remedies similar to those used by Shamans. He did not combine herbs and plants with prayers, rituals, or rites, but he did use them for healing and to help those around him live healthier lives. His spiritual depravity is what truly distinguishes him from Shamans and witches.

Galen of Pergamon was a Greek physician who pioneered the use of herbs. He made every effort to document all of his medical knowledge. This section contained a variety of works discussing herbs, plants, and their potential properties.

One of his most well-known books combined the use of herbs in medicine to not only improve people's health but also to aid in prevention. His knowledge and books aided medical professionals in calibrating medications so that they worked optimally for each individual. It demonstrated that each person is unique and must be treated as such.

Nicholas Culpeper is another name that conjures up images of herbal pioneers. He lived a brief but distinguished life and was frequently referred to as "the People's Herbalist." He had a tremendous impact on the world of herbology. Despite his influence, his peer group rejected him due to his views and beliefs in areas such as Astrology.

Culpeper was a physician with a passion for assisting the less fortunate. He spent the majority of his time researching and documenting the properties and characteristics of plants and herbs. He published numerous books, which were then translated into a variety of different languages. These books are still in use today and have enabled a large number of people to use herbal remedies from the moment they were written.

As a result of his adversity, he developed a genuine appreciation for and desire to assist those who were less fortunate. Not only did he provide medical services at a low or no cost, but he also counselled people on how to improve their health. His clients adored him because he dedicated his life to assisting those in need regardless of their financial situation.

Culpeper desired to educate people about the possibility of natural healing. He combined his knowledge of the pharmaceutical industry with his research on plants and herbs to provide people with health and healing options and information. He published a sizable number of books. They continue to be studied and used throughout the world today.

There was a time when natural healing through herbs was less popular; however, it has always existed and will continue to exist. The American Medical Foundation founded the Council on Medical Education, which contributed to herbalism's demise for a time. This group successfully campaigned to have herbalism removed from classrooms and many medical schools. Herbalism's popularity waned as a result of a lack of information available to students.

Herbalism's popularity has resurged. Herbs will never be completely eliminated from the table due to the healthy solutions they provide. Many people desire natural healing and believe it leads to a more fulfilling life. In today's society, information about herbs and their healing properties is much more accessible and will remain so regardless of their popularity.

While we have examined only a few of the world's herbal pioneers, it is critical to recognise that many others contributed. We will continue to grow and learn about herbs and plants, and as a result, herbal pioneers will exist. Simply because this is an ancient practise does not mean it will not evolve and change in the future. As it grows, people will continue to have an impact and will play a critical role in the advancement of herbal knowledge.

Correspondence with Plant Spirits

Previously, it was stated that plants possess a spirit or soul. Believe it or not, we have the ability to communicate with them. Historically, it was common for shamans to communicate with higher powers through plants. It aided in their alignment with the spirit world.

We were all once inextricably linked to the earth and natural world. It is less common in today's world, but it is possible. The shamans' spirituality and connection to plants survives today through folklore. Numerous healers, witches, and herbalists believe that our physical and emotional ailments are caused by disturbances in our emotional and spiritual bodies.

Plants are well-known for their ability to heal in these areas.

By developing a positive relationship with nature, plants, and herbs, we can reclaim our natural ability to heal. While these teachings are not as prevalent as they once were, they are unquestionably making a comeback. More people are discovering healthier and more fruitful lives as a result of their connection to natural rather than manmade things.

Not only do many people believe that we can communicate with plants, but they also believe that we can communicate with them. We can hear them calling if we listen closely. If you want to learn to hear nature's call, the best way to do so is to get outside and experience it. Taking time to go for a hike in a remote area of the wilderness is an excellent way to accomplish this.

As with anything magical, you must first establish your intention and maintain it while wandering through a natural setting. This intention will assist you in attracting the appropriate energies. Once you begin to hear the plants' call, you will gain a better understanding of their potent energy and healing properties.

When attempting to strengthen your connection with herbs and other plants, it is necessary to have not only a focused intention but also an offering. Plants will cooperate with you if they believe you are deserving. By presenting them with a gift, such as nutrients, you will find that they are more receptive to sharing information about healing and their other characteristics.

Another way to more easily connect with the spirit of plants is to treat them with respect. By showing love and respect for plants, you will increase their desire to communicate with you. Many people recognise that plants have feelings, and when we treat them with respect, compassion, and love, it's natural that they'll want to collaborate with us to heal and brighten the spirits and minds of those around them.

Another excellent way to connect with plants and their spirits is through nature meditation. Concentrated meditation enables you to truly take in your surroundings and can help you hear what the plants and herbs around you are trying to communicate. This is a process that requires time, patience, and practise. Bear in mind that with continued concentration, love, and intention, connecting with plant spirits can become quite simple.

CHAPTER 2:

BEGINNING THE PATH WITH HERBS

Chapter two will discuss where, to begin with, herbs. We'll compare purchasing herbs to growing them yourself or foraging for them in the wild. While most people achieve the greatest success with spellcasting by growing their own herbs, others prefer to purchase them.

Additionally, you will learn how to care for herbs whether you grow them at home or cultivate them in the wild. This includes instructions on how to create a garden in your own backyard, even if you have limited space. There are a few things to consider when gathering herbs in the wild, as well as certain herbs or plants to avoid; these will also be discussed.

Finally, you can gain valuable insight into the proper methods for gathering, drying, and storing your herbs. How you handle them will determine whether or not they are suitable for use in your magical practises. If done incorrectly, you can endanger the energy they hold, which can have a detrimental effect on your spells.

There are numerous plants and herbs available to you. Many people find it intimidating to attempt to determine where to begin. However, it does not have to be intimidating. There are a few essential herbs that every witch or Wiccan should have on hand at all times of the day.

Let's begin this chapter by examining ten different herbs that you should keep on hand at all times. They will aid in the casting of spells and the practise of magic. Many of them are likely already in your home, while others may require cultivation or investment. Bear in mind that the best method is to grow your own herbs or to collect them in the wild. If you lack a green thumb, however, purchasing them from a store is also acceptable.

Apple blossoms are an excellent item to have on hand. Throughout history, apples have been regarded as a symbol of immortality. Not only is it associated with immortality, but also with the dead. According to some mythical legends, an apple branch bearing fruit can act as a portal to the underworld. Apples are also frequently used in love magic. Additionally, it is wonderful for creating a variety of different brews, incense, and incantations.

Basil is the next herb that you'll want to stock up on. It possesses a variety of magical properties. It can be used in conjunction with purification and luck spells. Not only that, having a basil plant in your home attracts good fortune. Basil is an extremely adaptable herb. Additionally, it can be used in love spells and divination. It is truly convenient to have on hand.

If you're looking for a herb that is both protective and purifying, you should consider chamomile. Numerous people meditate with it. Additionally, it can be used to defend against psychological or magical attacks. When chamomile is incorporated into your incense, it can be extremely beneficial if you have been having difficulty sleeping. Chamomile is reputed to bring good fortune. This can be advantageous in gambling or when looking for a lover.

In general, this plant can be used to attract good fortune into your life.

Lavender is another essential herb to have on hand. It is frequently used in love spells. Additionally, lavender can assist you in achieving peace or calm in your life. It is frequently used in sachets. Additionally, you'll find it hanging around people's homes to ensure they don't have nightmares and get a good night's sleep.

Mugwort is a herb that is used in a variety of magical practises. It is frequently used in spell casting, incense making, and smudging. This herb is extremely adaptable and straightforward to grow. You will not require a green thumb to succeed. Divination requires the use of this herb. It assists in revealing prophecy to us through our dreams and meditation. Pregnant women should exercise caution when using Mugwort, as it has the potential to be harmful.

Patchouli is another popular herb that you should keep on hand. It is incorporated into a wide variety of spells and rituals. The scent assists in transporting our minds to other dimensions. It is associated with the casting of spells for wealth, love, and sexual prowess. Many people discover that its strength is excellent for attracting money into their lives. There are numerous spells that can be cast with this herb to assist you in overcoming financial difficulties. It is also beneficial in today's world for repelling negativity from our lives.

Pennyroyal is a herb that can be used for a variety of strength and protection spells. Pennyroyal is well-known for assisting in the elimination of malice from one's life. For protection, people frequently stuff sachets with this herb. It is small enough to carry around with you and will protect you from any negative energies that may come your way.

Additionally, it has a positive connotation of prosperity and wealth. You can create a variety of different drinks and soaps to help you earn money.

Rosemary is another common herb that most people already have in their homes. When it comes to improving your memory or brainpower, this herb is a must-have. Rosemary is used in a wide variety of religious rituals. Numerous cultures have discovered that it provides an excellent level of protection against evil spirits. It is frequently burned in the home to purify it. Additionally, it is extremely beneficial during meditation. You will notice that your concentration is improved. Rosemary is also hung on doors to ward off intruders.

The next common herb that you are likely to have on hand is sage. Sage is excellent for purifying your home or cleansing a space. Additionally, burning sage is frequently used in rituals. It was once used to impart wisdom and clarity to a person's mental state.

Carrying sage leaves can assist you in improving your financial situation.

Additionally, it can assist in guiding you through the spirit world. These are just a few of the numerous applications for sage. It is truly one of the most critical herbs to keep on hand.

Yarrow is another common herbal remedy that is extremely beneficial in magical practises.

It possesses tremendous healing properties and can be used in healing spells and a variety of healing ointments. Yarrow is frequently used in love and courage spells. It can be worn to boost one's self-esteem. Numerous individuals use it to assist them in overcoming their fears. Yarrow is used in both magical bathing and sachets.

This is just a sampling of the herbs you'll want to include in your magical arsenal. It's an excellent place to begin. You must understand that you have access to a large variety of herbs, and while many of them share similar properties, they are all unique in their own way.

It is beneficial to become familiar with the most frequently used herbs. It will take time, research, and dedication to master these magical herbs, but they will truly assist you in your quest for a healthier and happier life.

Purchasing vs. Growing Herbs

In this section, we'll discuss the distinctions between purchasing herbs and growing or collecting them yourself.

There are numerous divergent views on the optimal method of herb acquisition. In reality, growing them or collecting them from the wild will always be the best option.

When you visit your local grocery store, you will always find a good selection of different plants and herbs.

Occasionally, this is your only option. The disadvantage of purchasing herbs from a store is their low energy levels. Additionally, there may be issues with the way the plants were handled and raised, which could have an effect on their power when used for spellcasting.

When a plant is displayed in a store, it will come into contact with a variety of different people. They will leave an imprint of their energy on the plant, whether intentionally or unintentionally. This may have unfavourable consequences when you attempt to use it. If you purchased your herbs from a store, you can cleanse them to remove any negative energies. Indeed, it is critical that you cleanse them of any energies they may have absorbed prior to using them.

Because plants are highly sensitive, the environment in which they are grown has an effect on the amount of power they possess. If you purchase your plants and herbs from a store, it is likely that they received little attention when they were young and just beginning to grow. This could indicate that your energy levels are depleted. It is possible to charge your herbs and increase their energy level, and it is likely beneficial to do so if you purchase your herbs from a marketplace.

There are specialty stores where you can purchase fresh or dried herbs. These specialised stores are frequently devoted to witchcraft. If you purchase your herbs from this type of store, you are likely to have more success than if you purchase them from your neighbourhood grocery store.

However, keep in mind that when purchasing herbs from a specialty shop such as this, you may end up paying significantly more.

Additionally, you must bear in mind that, while the majority of people have good intentions, there are those who have nefarious ones. They may incorporate negative intent into the items they sell, which may have an adverse effect on you.

The best course of action is always to create a herb garden and grow your own plants. You will then be able to grow them not only with love, but also with purpose. The communication between you and the plants in your immediate vicinity will be improved. They will feel loved, and as a result, they will strengthen and provide you with increased levels of positive energy during your spellcasting practises.

You do not need to be an expert gardener to create a herb garden. Herbs are actually quite easy to grow. Additionally, establishing a herb garden does not require a large amount of space. It can be carried out in small apartments or on large expanses of land. It makes no difference. All you need is the motivation and desire to grow your own herbs.

If you truly do not wish to cultivate your own herbs, you can also gather them in the wild. You must exercise extreme caution and ensure that you are certain of what you are looking for. It is critical to understand the shape, size, smell, and location of specific herbs. Selecting the incorrect plant can have disastrous consequences. Certain herbs and plants may appear to be very similar but possess vastly different properties. What you may be using for a healing spell may actually end up harming you if you are unaware that it is a toxic plant.

Therefore, if you are going to venture into the wilderness, you will need to spend some time conducting research. To begin, you'll want to examine the plant species that grow nearby. Certain plants will only grow in specific regions of the world. Additionally, you must become acquainted with the plant as a whole. This will aid in its recognition while you are on the lookout for it.

In general, regardless of how you collect your herbs, it is critical that you develop a fundamental knowledge base about them. Understanding their properties and magical applications will assist you in selecting the appropriate items. Additionally, you should learn how to dry and store them. In a moment, we'll delve deeper into that.

Herbs Growing

Herb growing at home does not have to be difficult. This is the most advantageous method of cultivating these enchanted plants. Learning how to grow them at home will aid you in manifesting the spells you intend to cast. Your garden can be grown indoors or outdoors.

When you choose to create a garden that helps you connect with nature, you will also develop a stronger bond with your plants. It can assist you in communicating with them and comprehending the remedies they may be able to add to your life. You'll need an understanding of how plants grow and what you can do to ensure their success. Each herb will require a unique approach, so learning a few at a time will help you avoid becoming overwhelmed.

When you first begin learning how to grow herbs, one of the most beneficial things you can do is observe them in their natural environment. When you begin to examine them, they can have a profound effect. It facilitates communication with the plants and also has a calming effect. When you establish a connection with plants in their natural habitat, it will be much easier to establish a connection with them once they are in your home.

Another advantage of observing plants grow in their natural environment is that you can observe what happens in their environment. It can indicate whether they require a lot of sun, a lot of water, or a lot of shade. When you bring plants into your home, the vibes you experience when you are around them in their natural environment will easily transfer to them.

After encountering herbs in their natural environment, it's time to bring them into your home. Seeds and pre-started plants are available at a variety of different locations. It's critical to remember that starting your plants from seeds is the optimal way to grow them, as this ensures that you'll be cultivating them from the moment they sprout. From the moment they are planted, you can infuse them with good intentions and positive energy.

One of the primary concerns that people have about growing herbs at home is a lack of space. This may appear to be a challenge, particularly if you live in a small apartment. However, regardless of where you live, there are a variety of different ways to grow herbs at home.

If you have a limited amount of space, one option is to grow your herbs in pots. There are numerous pots of various sizes that can be easily placed on shelves near windows or on windowsills. Pots do not take up a lot of space, which makes them ideal for a small space. Having a potted plant garden in your home will provide you with both comfort and the necessary herbs for a variety of different Wiccan practises.

Another possibility is to purchase window boxes. When you live in a small space, you can hang window boxes outside each window to provide ample planting space. You must exercise caution here, as some herbs do not require a lot of sunlight, while others do. Thus, location is critical to ensuring that they receive an adequate amount of sunlight throughout the day.

Naturally, if you have more space, creating a garden will be easier. Plants thrive when they are outdoors. Therefore, if you have an outside space suitable for gardening, this will be the most advantageous. Some people prefer raised gardens because they look very nice in terms of landscaping. Others prefer to create a more traditional garden. In either case, it is perfectly acceptable as long as you provide an abundance of love and attention to the herbs you are attempting to grow.

After you've grown your herbs, you'll need to harvest them. It is critical to note that dried herbs are available in a variety of different stores. Again, growing your own and drying them yourself will provide you with herbs that are more potent than those purchased in a store. Additionally, herbs purchased at a grocery store go bad quickly, so you'll need to use them quickly. When you drive them at home, they typically have a longer shelf life.

Generally, you'll gather your herbs in bunches. Simply tie a string around the bunch's base and hang it upside down to dry. There are other methods for drying herbs; however, this is the most secure method. While it is advantageous to look up each herb individually to determine how they should be dried, this is the method you will use the majority of the time.

After your herbs have dried, they must be stored. There are numerous methods for storing herbs. At the end of the day, all that is required is that they are stored in an airtight container. Many people prefer to store herbs in glass jars.

Glass jars are probably your best bet, as they will preserve your dried herbs the longest.

If you are unable to cultivate a garden at home, you can gather them from the wild. We briefly discussed this previously. When foraging for herbs in the wild, you must exercise extreme caution and have a strong foundation of knowledge about herbs.

Numerous plants have a similar appearance, which can be dangerous.

You may believe you are purchasing one thing but end up with a poisonous plant. Clearly, this is something to avoid.

If you choose to collect herbs in the wild, it is beneficial to invest in a book that will assist you in identifying them. Books can teach you the small details that make identifying the correct herb easier. Along with learning about the herbs you're looking for, you should familiarise yourself with the herbs native to your region. Numerous herbs are endemic to a particular region of the world. This means that if you require additional herbs, you must purchase them from a store or nursery.

CHAPTER 3:

CHARGING HERBS, HERBAL BATHING, & HERBAL TEAS

This chapter teaches you how to infuse your herbs with positive energy so that they can be used in spellcasting. By charging your herbs, you can increase the effectiveness of your manifesting spells. It is not time consuming, but it is a necessary step in the process.

After discussing charging, we'll discuss herbal bathing.

When you take baths with herbs added, a variety of different spells and positive outcomes occur. Not only will we discuss herbal bathing, but we'll also provide you with a couple of spells to use during these baths.

Finally, we will discuss herbal teas. Tea is an excellent medium for divination spells. Additionally, you can use them to cast spells for energy, luck, and prosperity. It's incredible what a cup of herbal tea can do for the mind, body, and spirit.

Energizing Herbs

Charging your herbs is critical to ensuring that they retain sufficient power for spellcasting. When you plant your seeds or starter plants for the first time, they must be charged. If you do not charge them now, you must do so before using them for magical purposes. Certain individuals prefer to charge them at both steps to ensure they have the maximum amount of energy possible. This should be accomplished through the use of your own magical energy. Charging your herbs is not a difficult or time-consuming process, but it is critical.

Take your herbs outside and sit on the ground to charge them. You should then clear your mind and personally send her. Additionally, spending time grounding your root chakra is beneficial. This will enable you to connect with the energy of the Earth beneath you. Begin a simple meditation focused on infusing your body with positive earth energy. This should be done while holding the herb or seed plants in your hands.

As you concentrate on the energy entering your body, you should notice it moving within you and toward the herbs you are holding. Certain individuals prefer to use mantras to ensure that their energy is combined with that of the plants or seeds.

Additionally, you should charge your herbs if you are using dried herbs that have been sitting for a while. After being dried, a herb loses some of its energy, which must be replaced. Fresh herbs that have recently been dried have a higher concentration of NRG, so if you charged them prior to planting them, you likely won't need to worry about this step when using them for spellcasting.

The procedure for recharging dried herbs is identical. It all comes down to intention, focus, and meditation. Additionally, you can increase the flow of positive energy by utilising tools such as crystals and candles. Later in this book, we'll discuss candles and crystals, and how they can aid you in casting herbal spells.

Bathing with Herbal Extracts

Bathing with herbs is frequently referred to as ritual bathing. It is critical because it can help you boost your magical energy and put you in the proper frame of mind to perform a variety of magical practises. It aids in the elimination of negative energy from the mind, body, and soul. Herbal bathing has been practised for generations and will continue to be a significant aspect of herbal magic in the future.

Herbal bathing is frequently used for purification. It can assist in calming and relaxing you. Additionally, herbal baths have incredible healing properties. Aromas are extremely therapeutic and have a spiritual effect on people like few other things. Additionally, it can assist you in achieving balance.

Herbal bathing has a plethora of benefits. On a physical level, it can assist you in improving circulation, resolving sleep problems, and maintaining healthy skin. Mentally, it can help you cope with stress and anxiety. After participating in herbal bathing, you will feel more relaxed, calm, and warm. Additionally, it will strengthen your connection to and awareness of the more spiritual side of things.

It is not difficult to create a herbal bath. Generally, all you need to do is add a variety of different herbs to your bathtub. At other times, you will need to bring water to a boil and add the herbs to extract their oils and energy. This is not always necessary; it simply depends on your objective.

If you're looking for protection or purification, you can create a very simple bath. Basil must be steeped in 1 cup of boiling water. After steeping, strain the herb from the water. Simply add it to your bathwater from there. Once in the bathtub, you must relax and meditate with the intention of being protected or purified. After completing this bathing ritual, you should allow your body to dry naturally. By blotting away excess moisture with a towel, you can reduce the efficacy of this bathing ritual.

Another wonderful spell that can be performed with herbal bathing is to assist in cleansing the negative energies that have become attached to you. To begin, you will need to cast a circle in your bathroom. You should invoke the elements and light a couple of lavender-colored candles.

This spell is a little more difficult to perform because you will need to create a sachet. A sachet is a small bag that contains a variety of items. This one requires dried and crushed chamomile, lavender, and rosemary. Simply hang it over your faucet and run your bath from there. Water will flow over the sachet, infusing your bath with the beneficial properties of these enchanted herbs. After drawing the bath, add approximately 1/2 cup lemon juice.

Immerse yourself in warm bathwater and unwind. Concentrate on your breathing. Visualize, with your eyes closed, that the stress, tension, and negative energy are evaporating from your body. Enter a meditative state and maintain your focus on releasing negativity.

Several minutes should be spent in this meditative state.

Once you feel relaxed and free of the negativity that has been weighing on you, you can exit the bathtub. Again, rather than towelling off, you should allow your body to dry naturally. This increases the spell's effectiveness. It is critical to note that you will need to thoroughly clean your bathtub to ensure that no residue is left behind. This will also ensure that all negative energy is completely removed from your life.

If your life has recently become chaotic, taking a herbal bath for peace may be beneficial. There are numerous bathing practises that can help bring peace to your surroundings, and we're going to share one of our favourites with you. This bath has more steps than others, so take your time and concentrate on what you were doing throughout each step.

To begin, run your bath and add about a tablespoon of milk. Following that, you should add 6 to 8 rose petals. It makes no difference whether they are fresh or dried. With your fingers, move the rose petals and milk around your bathtub.

After adding these ingredients and mixing them together, you should say something along the lines of "Water ripples in the wind, pollen moves through the air, more silent than a peaceful sea, a burning desire to bring peace here." This will assist in sustaining the tranquillity you seek in your life.

After a few moments of chanting this mantra, you can enter the magical herbal bath you have created. Additionally, lighting some white candles can help increase the spell's power. While in the bath, reflect on the fact that you no longer desire chaos in your life. Concentrate your intention on peace. Allow the water to draw negative energies away from you and replace them with the tranquillity of the herb mixture.

After several minutes of meditation on finding peace in your life, you can exit the bathtub. As with other ritual baths, you should allow sufficient time for your skin to dry naturally. Drain and clean the tub to rid yourself of the mayhem that has consumed your life. Collect the rose petals and bury them in a location far from your home. You're certain to notice a new sense of calm surrounding you and your home from here.

While there are numerous herbal baths that can be used for magical purposes, we'll look at one more. This is a bath that can assist in the infusion of love into your life. Love spells are among the most popular, but they are also among the most dangerous. You must exercise caution when considering the possibility of casting love spells. This is a bit safer, as it merely serves to open you up to the possibility of love. You will not actually be casting a love spell on another person.

To create a bath that will enhance your attractiveness, fill your bathtub halfway with warm water. It is critical that the temperature does not exceed 90 degrees. 4 to 5 navel oranges will be added from there. Additionally, you should include a bunch of fresh mint leaves. After that, you'll enter the bathtub.

After soaking in the tub, peel the oranges and squeeze the juice into the water. You should rub the peels and fruit directly onto your skin and hair. Following that, you should repeat the procedure with the mint leaves. Many people enjoy chewing on a mint leaf to amp up the effectiveness of this spell.

After completing these steps, you must enter a relaxed state of meditation. As is the case with all spells, your intent must be crystal clear. This value should be centred on the fact that you want to increase your attractiveness to the people who are meant to bring you love. Concentrate and meditate for as long as possible on this aspect. This procedure should be repeated several times consecutively.

After several minutes of contemplation, you may exit the bathtub. Allow your body to dry naturally rather than using a towel. You are not required to keep any of the fruit or herbs that you have placed in the bathtub; simply discard them. As you continue to use this herbal bath, you will notice that you are more irresistible than ever.

Teas with Herbs

After discussing the incredible benefits of herbal bathing, we're going to discuss herbal teas. Throughout history, herbal teas have been used for a variety of different purposes.

Additionally, herbal teas are consumed in nearly every culture on the planet. While teas are delicious and soothing to drink, they also possess a plethora of magical properties. Through the use of herbal teas, you can achieve divination, increased luck in life, and prosperity.

Tease magic is extremely powerful. It is capable of casting spells and endowing us with the ability of divination. When tea magic is practised, they tend to be calm and powerful. The herbs they use enable them to easily centre themselves and gain insight and enlightenment about both the visible and invisible worlds.

Tea is not only consumed as a beverage. Numerous and individuals also use it to create sachets and stuff their pillows. It can help you sleep better and allows you to create a variety of different charms.

When tea magic is used, negative thoughts and energies can be easily removed.

While the majority of herbal teas are made from the same leaves, there are numerous varieties of tea. Additionally, various plant parts are utilised to add to the variety. Certain teas will have more potent or superior magical properties depending on their intended use.

There are a few distinct methods by which tea is prepared, and a herbalist will easily distinguish them. Some are grown on the summits of mountains, while others thrive in proximity to large bodies of water.

The type of tea you use will depend on the outcome you desire. The season also has an effect on the type of tea you should choose for your magical purpose.

Black tea is well-known for its ability to instil courage in its drinker.

Additionally, it can be beneficial if you are bored, as it will add excitement to your life. This type of tea is most frequently used to cast spells to attract money into one's life. Additionally, it can stimulate your mind, making you more aware of your surroundings.

If you're looking to attract money into your life through black tea, magic can be extremely beneficial. One spell that you can use is quite straightforward. Before you place the teabag in your glass of hot water, you will hold it between both hands. While holding it, visualise money entering your life. Consider how you will acquire wealth and how you will use it. Concentrate on happiness and wealth. After infusing your black tea with your intent, steep it in water while maintaining your focus on the outcome you wish to manifest. Continue drinking your tea normally from there. Repeating this process several days in a row will assist in ensuring that money comes your way.

Additionally, oolong tea possesses a variety of magical properties. It is well-known for assisting in the development of serenity and love in a person's life. Additionally, it can assist you in reflecting on your past in order to help bring emotional balance to your future. Additionally, this type of tea is excellent if you are engaged in divination practises or attempting to foretell the future.

Numerous people employ oolong tea in love spells. Again, you will need to hold the teabag between both of your hands and meditate and visualise the presence of love in your life. Take the time to truly envision your ideal partner's appearance and behaviour. The more specifics you can come up with, the better. This includes imagining how it will feel when they touch you and how you will react when they are close by. Throughout this procedure, you will require complete and intense concentration. The meditation process should be extended beyond what is considered normal.

After infusing your intention into the tea bag, steep it in hot water and drink it. You must continue casting this tea spell in order to attract love into your life.

Tea leaf divination is extremely common. It is one of the best exercises you can do to improve your divination abilities. Tea leaf reading is an ancient tradition that will endure for future generations. When you read tea leaves, you are interpreting the symbols formed by the leaves. While not as popular as crystal reading or tarot, this method of divination is still widely used. Tea leaf divination is not as popular as it once was due to the high margin of error. It is not a fully understood act, and our perception of a pattern may be quite different from someone else's. Naturally, when we perceive things differently, we will interpret them differently.

When it comes to divination via tea leaves, it's all about focusing your energy. All magic originates with your intention. You should infuse the tea with your intention, which will allow them to reveal the signs of whatever question you are seeking answers to. It is capable of providing glimpses into the past, present, or future. There are numerous texts available that can assist you in deciphering what the symbol on your tea leaves is attempting to communicate.

When working with divination via tea leaf reading, there is a process that must be followed. To begin, brew a cup of tea. Your teacup should be of a light hue. Additionally, you must use loose tea leaves, not tea leaves enclosed in a bag. It is critical to note that simply opening a tea bag will not suffice.

They use leaves that are far too fine to form obvious patterns.

Following the preparation of your cup of tea, you should take some time to reflect on your intentions. It is most advantageous to do this while holding the cup. It enables your energy to be transferred to the tea leaves contained within your cup. Regardless of who is seeking answers, what matters most is the intent of the person performing the divination. Your question should be succinct.

You should begin sipping the tea once the water has cooled to a drinkable temperature. While drinking it, you must constantly visualise and focus on the question at hand. You should consume all of the tea except about a tablespoon. Leaves will eventually settle to the bottom. From here, hold the cup in your hand and swirl it three times clockwise.

After three swirls, flip the cup over onto a saucer. It should hold this position for approximately a minute. After that, you'll rotate it three more times. Return the cup to an upright position by flipping it over. Tea leaves should be adhered to the cup in a variety of shapes. This is the point at which we should look into them and read the story they have to tell.

You will need to invest some time and research into the appearance and meaning of various symbols in order to properly perform divination through tea leaf reading. It's a lot of work, but the results are absolutely incredible. Whether you are performing divination for yourself or for others, it has the potential to provide you with true insight into the future. As is the case with everything, practise makes perfect. Therefore, do not be discouraged. Simply keep practising, and reading your leaves will become easier over time.

CHAPTER 4:

SACHETS & ESSENTIAL OILS

Chapter four will discuss these fascinating magical practises. We'll begin by discussing magical sachets. Sachets are a multipurpose item that can be used for a variety of purposes. We will discuss their significance and demonstrate how to create a variety of different sachets and their associated uses.

Additionally, there will be information on essential oils. While you can purchase essential oils almost anywhere, you are more than likely purchasing an infusion rather than an actual essential oil. There are a variety of ways to make your own at home. We'll go over the process of creating your own essential oils and the purposes for which they're useful in magical practises.

Sachets

Additionally, sachets are referred to as charm bags. These are a simple method of creating and casting a spell while keeping it contained in a simple bag. A sachet can contain a variety of different items. It is entirely dependent on the spell you are attempting to cast. Herbs, essential oils, stones, crystals, and amulets can all be included.

These bags are incredibly simple to construct. Typically, they are constructed from a square of fabric that is tied together. Occasionally, individuals will use an embroidered cloth or will draw markings indicating their intention on the outside of the sachet. It can be constructed from a variety of materials. The most common material is burlap or cotton; however, they have been made from leather, silk, and a variety of other fabrics. To be honest, the fabric itself is secondary to the spell contained within.

Additionally, the colour of your sachet bag has an effect on the success of your spell. Let's take a moment to consider how different coloured bags can aid you in casting the spell you're attempting.

Obviously, we will not cover every colour on the spectrum, but we will cover the most popular ones.

A gold-colored sachet will assist in the empowerment of spells used to attract wealth into your life. They're also useful if you're looking for personal or property protection. If you're attempting to connect with the universe's higher powers, a gold-colored sachet will also work.

Utilizing a silver piece of cloth will assist in amplifying a prosperity spell. Silver is also fantastic for moon magic. If you're looking to boost your psychic abilities or connect with female higher powers, silver is the way to go.

When creating a healing sachet, you'll want to use a yellow piece of cloth. This colour is also beneficial if you are having difficulty finding work or if you require additional resources in your life. While not as common, a yellow cloth can also be used to infuse your home with warmth and happiness.

After that, we'll discuss orange. Utilizing an orange covering can help facilitate communication spells. Orange is also the colour associated with the throat chakra, which is the seat of your ability to communicate with yourself and others. An orange sachet can aid in the transmission of messages. Additionally, it can aid in the promotion of astral travel and astral projection.

Green is a very popular sachet colour. It encompasses a broad range of distinct desires and requirements. If you're looking for prosperity, you'll want to cover your sachet with a green sachet. It's also fantastic for cultivating friendships and relationships.

Green sachets can help you connect more deeply with the abundant energy that nature provides.

To create a charm that will bring justice to a difficult situation, purple cloth will be required. Purple sachets are also beneficial when seeking higher levels of wisdom or resolving life's mysteries. It can also assist in bringing wealth to you during times of financial difficulty.

Sachets made of red cloth will enhance the romance in your life. Red cloth is also an excellent choice if you're looking for strength. You will also be able to achieve success in your daily life with that strength. Numerous protection spells are also contained within red sachets.

If you are having difficulty with friendships, using a pink cloth for your sachet is beneficial. Additionally, the pink fabric will assist in opening your heart to love and allowing love to find you. Not only that, but there are a variety of different healing spells that are easier to manifest when the sachet's outer covering is pink.

Finally, but certainly not least, is the black sashay. A black outer covering is extremely effective at eliminating negative energies from your life. It is capable of absorbing any hexes that may be cast against you. Additionally, it assists in relieving stress and anxiety caused by the nefarious intentions of others.

Again, this is only a sampling of the numerous colours that could be used when creating a magical sachet. Almost always, one of these colours will work perfectly well. Bear in mind that the majority of bags will close with a drawstring, allowing you to open them and add materials if necessary. On rare occasions, you will completely seal a sachet; however, this is not the norm.

When designing a sachet, this shape should also be considered. If you're working on a love spell, it makes sense to shape it as a heart. This is not the most critical component, but it can boost the potency of your sachet and ensure that the spell you are casting manifests completely.

Now that you have a working knowledge of what a sachet is, let us proceed. We're going to give you some ideas for different types of sachets you can create from here. We'll examine sachets for good fortune, protection, love, and health.

When creating a sachet for a luck spell, you should use a bag that is either gold, green, or silver in colour. They will all work admirably to assist you in accomplishing your objective. Once the bag is created, the contents may vary, but some good items to consider include the following:

Herbs:

Clover

Nutmeg

Fenugreek

Ginger

Stones:

Green Agate

Sunstone with Tiger's Eye

Extras:

Grass of Spain

Grass of Ireland

Small Horseshoe (Alternatively, you can draw or paint a horseshoe on the sachet's exterior material.)

Once you've assembled this sachet, you'll need to infuse it with your intent. This is easiest to accomplish in a meditative state.

Concentrate your thoughts and envision what your life will be like once your luck improves. Many people like to incorporate a mantra into this type of luck spell as well. You could say something along the lines of, "Fortune and fortune find me this day; for everything I seek is coming my way."

Protection is a universal need, and sashays are excellent at assisting us in obtaining it. This can be safeguarded against a variety of different threats. It can assist us in warding off negative energies that surround us.

Additionally, those with malice toward us can have their practises thwarted by the use of a magical sachet. To make a protection sachet, you'll need a black, red, or gold bag. It should be brimming with the following:

Herbs

Cedar

Mint

Cinnamon

Betony

Gems:

Amber

Black Tourmaline

Additional Malachite:

 A Sea Shell

A Snippet of Straw Broom

After creating a sachet, intention and meditation are always involved.

Throughout the creation process, you should keep your mind on the reason for the creation. After it is created, taking time to meditate on it and channel the appropriate energy into it will always be beneficial and will ensure that the manifestation of your outcome occurs properly. Finding a mantra or a prayer to incorporate into these sachets is also a good idea. One that will work well with this protection sachet is, "Dark energies must leave my space, and light will replace them."

Many people also desire love sachets. They will not only assist in bringing love into your life, but will also enable you to accept it if you are fearful of it. Love sachets are a gentle way to infuse your life with love. They are not nearly as dangerous as many other love spells you may have researched previously. You must exercise caution when dealing with personal matters. To create a love spell sachet, you'll need a pink or red bag.

It should include the following:

Herbs:

Rose Petals

Sticks of Cinnamon

Lavender

Gems:

Pink Kunzite

Quartz rose

Additional Materials: Maple Leaves

While you are meditating and imprinting your intention onto this sachet, you should concentrate on the type of love you wish to bring into your life. If you're looking for intimate love, you should concentrate on the characteristics of your ideal partner. If you're looking for friendship, you should consider the qualities that are most important to you in a friend. Throughout your meditations, you should repeat the following prayer or mantra: "With the four elements of earth, air, fire, and water, please allow the powers that be to bring love forward and on to me."

Finally, but certainly not least, we will teach you how to make a sachet that will aid in your health improvement. This includes not only physical health, but also mental and spiritual well-being. When seeking healing of any kind, a sachet made of blue or yellow material is recommended. Fill your blue or yellow sachet with the following:

Herbs:

Thyme

St. John's Wort (Hypericum perforatum)

Peppermint

Gems:

Sunstone

Amethyst

Toadstone

Extras: Sun Symbol

Your meditation should be healing-oriented. You should envision yourself as physically, mentally, and spiritually strong. Consider yourself overcoming incredible mental and physical challenges. Additionally, as is customary, you should direct your intention toward the sachet as you hold it in your hands. The mantra, "Healing my mind, body, and spirit so that they are fit and strong will strengthen my heart and enable my body to continue," is an excellent one for completing the task of creating an effective healing sachet.

Once you've created a sachet for your intended use, you can either wear it or sleep with it nearby. The more frequently you keep it nearby, the more effective it will be.

It can be carried in a pocket, purse, or simply kept in a frequented location. Sachets contain extremely potent magic, and the energy contained within them can be amplified by continuously meditating with them.

Aromatherapy Essential Oils

Essential oils have played a significant role in Wiccan rituals and magical practise for an extended period of time. Traditional magical practises involving the use of essential oils assist in bringing the positive energies of nature into your life. Additionally, it can assist in manifesting the change you seek.

Throughout recorded history, priests, healers, and shamans have used scented oils in magical rituals and medicine. They are combined with incense, tinctures, appointments, and charms and can be used for almost anything.

Essential oils can be derived from a variety of different sources.

This can include the entire plant. While it does require some effort and dedication to create your own essential oils, you will not receive the best results from those created by you. You can purchase essential oils from a variety of sources; however, not all essential oils are genuine.

They are frequently simple infusions of a herb or a plant with another oil. They are not the oils extracted from the plants themselves.

This is one of the primary reasons why it is advantageous to create your own essential oils.

While essential oils can play a significant role in casting spells, they are rarely the focal point. They are used to anoint a wide variety of ritualistic implements. This category encompasses crystals, talismans, and amulets. The use of essential oils also enhances candle magic. In reality, if you want to add energy to your spells and enhance them, the use of essential oils will provide you with the strength you seek.

If you attempt to purchase genuine essential oils, the cost can be quite high. Making them yourself can undoubtedly save you money. Compiling a good collection of these magical oils may take some time, but the effort will be well worth it. You must exercise caution when purchasing essential oils to ensure that they are 100% pure plant oils. Often, people will start with an oil base and add plant materials. This is not a true essential oil, but an infusion.

The issue is not limited to infusions. Regrettably, a large number of synthetically processed products are labelled as essential oils.

These are not made with plant-based materials, but rather with random oils and common sense. These would be useless if you attempted to use them in conjunction with spellcasting. As a result, many witches prefer to make their own essential oils, despite the fact that it is a lengthy process.

One fairly simple method for creating your own essential oils is to use a crockpot. Fill your crockpot halfway with the plant of your choice.

It will be beneficial to strip the leaves from the stems and cut the stems into small pieces. Many people also prefer to rip the leaves, as this facilitates the extraction of the oils.

After approximately halfway filling your crockpot with your plant, you will add water. Water should reach approximately an inch above the plant material. You should still have a reasonable amount of space at the crockpot's top. Instead of putting the lid on normally, you will do so upside down. This will allow the steam to easily escape the crockpot.

Once this is complete, you'll turn your crockpot to high. Allow it to remain on high for approximately one to two hours. Then you can reduce the heat to low in the crockpot. Allow it to cook for approximately four more hours on the lowest setting.

After four hours, turn off the crockpot and allow the mixture to cool completely. After it has cooled completely, place the entire crockpot in the refrigerator. Allow it to sit for at least one night.

It is critical that you carefully follow this step. If you place your crockpot in the refrigerator while it is still hot, it may crack or cause damage.

You'll be able to remove your mixture from the refrigerator the following day. What you were going to notice is that an oily white residue has now accumulated on the surface of the water. It should be quite difficult. You will need to carefully and quickly remove this oil. It will begin to melt in your hands if you do not act quickly. The essential oils that you collect can be placed in virtually any type of bottle. The bottle should include a lid and glasses, which is typically what people look for when purchasing dropper bottles. Ensure that each container is labelled so that you know what each bottle contains.

As you can see, making essential oils requires some time.

However, it is not as difficult as it appears. This is why the majority of people would rather make their own. Additionally, you can energise and imbue each oil with your intention as you create it. Storing them in a dark-colored glass container prevents them from spoiling and allows them to retain their energy for a longer period of time.

When first beginning to create essential oils, it is best to start with single oils.

However, as the Azure collection expands, you can create blends. The procedure is identical except that you will use two distinct types of plant matter rather than just one. After assembling a blend of essential oils, you should allow it to sit for a while before using it. This will give their energies the time they require to truly merge.

We have only shown you one method for creating your own essential oils. It is one of the simplest methods for doing so at home. Essentially, everyone has a crockpot lying around, so it will be simple and will not require a significant investment. Keep in mind, however, that there are a variety of other ways to create your own essential oils.

There are numerous books and articles on the subject, and it would only take a little research to find another route if this one isn't particularly interesting. Bear in mind that this is one of the simplest methods and will guarantee that you are receiving pure essential oils.

CHAPTER 5:

BASIC HERBS & BEGINNER SPELLS

In Chapter 2, we discussed ten essential herbs that everyone should have on hand. Obviously, there are numerous other herbs that will complement your magical practises. This chapter will discuss the best herbs to use for magical practises. While some of the ten herbs discussed previously will be included, we have also included a few others that are excellent starting herbs.

Additionally, this chapter will include spells for each herb discussed previously. These are intended for beginners. Each spell will be quite simple to perform. There will be spells to aid you in achieving success, wealth, good fortune, prosperity, love, anxiety, pain, and reproductive health. There is truly a spell for everyone that can assist with almost any situation. This is particularly true when it comes to herbal spells.

The first herb we'd like to discuss is sage. Sage possesses a variety of magical properties that can be extremely beneficial to you and your life. It is well-known for its efficacy in cleansing and healing spells.

Additionally, it is beneficial to use it when cleansing ritual tools or banishing evil from your life. Sage is also excellent for gaining wisdom or gaining a better understanding of a difficult situation. It can assist in relieving pain and allowing you to absorb the lessons life has to teach us.

One of the most frequently performed spells with a sage bundle is to purify an area of evil spirits. If you believe your home is haunted or that someone has cast a hex on you, burning sage can be an excellent way to deal with it. This spell is incredibly simple to perform. All you need is a sage bundle and a strong intention. If a particular area of your home appears to have a higher level of negativity than others, that is where you should begin. Circulate around the room, wafting the sage smoke in all directions. While you are doing this, you should be intent on banishing the malevolent energies that surround you and your life. It is critical to pay special attention to the doorways that connect rooms.

Bay Laurel is another herb with a plethora of magical properties. It is capable of providing a user with prophecy visions. Additionally, it can bring clarity to their lives. Numerous people have been known to use Bay Laurel in cleansing and purification spells. It can assist a person in achieving success and attracting positive energy into their lives. Additionally, it is beneficial for manifesting wishes and bringing love into one's life.

If you're attempting to cast a spell for prophetic dreams, Bay Laurel will assist you. Whatever question you are attempting to answer should be scribbled on a blank sheet of white paper. After you've jotted down your question, brew a cup of Bay Laurel tea. Proceed to your bedroom with the tea and your question. Please place the newspaper next to your bed on the floor.

After placing it there, drink the freshly brewed tea and refocus your attention on the conundrum at hand. Your question should be answered before you fall asleep. After you've received an answer to your question, you should burn the piece of paper on which you wrote it. This pays tribute to the prophetic spirits who aided you on your path toward understanding.

Rosemary also possesses a plethora of magical properties. If you're looking to cast a spell for beauty, rejuvenation, or love, this one has a variety of beneficial properties. Additionally, it is known to be beneficial for protection and purification spells. If you're in need of empowerment or clarity in a difficult situation, Rosemary is an excellent herb with which to cast a spell. When working with Rosemary, a great tip is to burn a few of its leaves prior to casting any spells. It will enable you to unwind and cleanse your surroundings prior to casting a spell. Additionally, you will notice that after burning a few of these leaves, you will be free of nightmares. Rosemary is excellent for promoting positive dreams.

Following that, let's discuss basil. Basil possesses magical properties that can assist you in attracting luck and wealth into your life. Additionally, it is effective in a variety of different types of love spells. Spells that incorporate basil will assist in bringing an abundance of blessings into a person's life. Additionally, it has been discovered that spells utilising basil can aid in clarity, protection, and purification.

If your financial situation has been less than ideal recently, basil can assist in bringing money into your life. This is one of the simplest spells to create. As with anything, intent is critical. To cast a basil spell to attract money into your life, all you need is a basil leaf. On the leaf, you should draw a money symbol. After you've drawn the symbol on it, hold the leaf between your two hands. Locate a peaceful location and meditate with the leaf held loosely in your hands. Obviously, you must direct your intention toward the quality of your life and the appearance of your life once you receive money. After you've completed your meditation session, simply place the leaf inside your wallet. Several days of meditation on this leaf will assist in amplifying the power of your spell.

Another essential herb that everyone should have on hand is lavender.

It is frequently used in spells designed to attract love, beauty, good fortune, and attraction into one's life. Additionally, it is excellent if someone has malice toward you or if you need to protect yourself from negativity. It can be extremely effective when you need to expel nefarious entities from your life and protect yourself or your home.

Many people strive to find love. Lavender can undoubtedly assist you in this endeavour. Women will have a greater chance of success with this love spell than men will with women. To use lavender in a love spell, you will need to create a sachet. A good example of one to make is sachets, which are discussed in detail in the chapter. After you've created the sachet, you'll want to infuse it with your loving intentions. Concentrate on your ideal mate.

Consider what it would be like to be around them and how you would both feel afterward. After you've completed your meditation, place the sachet beneath your pillow. Spend seven nights with it here. Each night, complete the same meditation before placing it beneath your pillow. After you've done this, you'll notice that love begins to enter your life quite quickly.

It is entirely possible to increase the power of this spell.

Lavender essential oils, soaps, and incense all contain lavender. It is preferable to make your own lavender essential oils if you intend to use them. By combining all three of these products, you can amp up the power of the love spell that was cast. A few drops of lavender essential oil on your sachet and wrists will amp up the potency. Using lavender-scented soap on your body and burning lavender-scented incense throughout your home will also assist in empowering this spell.

Following that, we'll discuss vanilla. Vanilla is ideal if you're attempting to increase your sensuality. Additionally, it is beneficial for seduction and love spells. Vanilla is well-known for its use in spells for peace, good fortune, and business enhancement. Additionally, you can use it when attempting to achieve prophetic or lucid dreams. Vanilla has a plethora of magical applications.

Every now and then, we all reach a point in our lives when we feel a little down. If you're looking for a good spell to bring happiness to your home and life, vanilla may be the answer.

To create this spell, you will need a powdered vanilla bean and sugar mixture. It should be stored in a tightly sealed glass jar. Simply by placing this jar in a window of your home, you will attract happiness and peace. Additionally, you will notice that your level of affection is amplified. This mixture can be used as a body scrub to amplify the effects of this happiness spell.

Another fantastic spell that you can easily cast using vanilla will aid in the growth of your business. Profitability is critical in business. If you find that you are in need of additional income to sustain your life, a vanilla spell will assist you in obtaining that additional income. You will need a fluffy piece of cotton to cast this spell. Using vanilla oil and a few drops of Wintergreen essential oil, soak the cotton. Sprinkle a teaspoon of cinnamon over the cotton. Place the cotton near the area in your business where money is stored. Spend some time meditating on your intention for not only the cotton swab but also the area where you keep your money. Once you've established your intent, you'll notice that money begins to flow into your business almost immediately.

Patchouli is another plant that possesses a number of magical properties. It has been used in spells intended to attract prosperity and wealth into one's life. Patchouli is also beneficial when seeking lust or true love. Numerous people frequently use this herb when casting fertility spells. There are numerous spells that can be cast with this herb, and these are just a sampling of them. It is a necessary herb to have on hand.

This herb is ideal for use in a herbal bath spell for fertility. To accomplish this, place a pink candle inside a green candle near your bathtub. Additionally, you should have a seven-day candle scented with natural patchouli. After that, run a bath and add approximately ten drops of patchouli essential oil. Then, in the bathwater, add a few drops of lemon essential oil, orange essential oil, and lime essential oil. While lighting the candles and standing in the bathtub, keep your focus on your intention. Fill a container halfway with water and pour it over your head. Continue drenching your body with water until you are completely submerged.

Relax in the bathtub. From here, you'll want to enter the most profound level of meditation possible. Consider how your pregnancy will be. You should also consider how you will feel when the baby is born. Concentrating on the candle flames can assist you in achieving the state of relaxation necessary for this level of meditation. You must maintain the meditation for 15–20 minutes. After that, exit the bathtub and allow your body to air dry. Repetition of this spell for seven days will put you well on your way to becoming pregnant.

Now we'll discuss apple blossoms. Apple blossoms are associated with an astounding variety of different magical properties. Oftentimes, people will use these wonderful smelling flowers in conjunction with love spells. Additionally, they are excellent for healing rituals. Many people believe that if you're attempting to make contact with the goddess, these blossoms can assist you. They are quite spiritual in nature, which means they will strengthen your connection to higher powers and the universe.

Apple blossom love spells are extremely popular. Consider one that can assist you in reintroducing love or romance into your life after a period of absence. Begin by surrounding yourself with pink and red candles. They should be in the shape of a circle. In the centre, you will sit cross-legged. To begin, light the candles and hold an apple blossom branch between your two hands. Remove the petals from the flower as you concentrate your intent.

Sprinkle the Flowers in a clockwise motion around you. While doing so, you must maintain your focus and send your intention out into the world. Utilize a mantra such as "Apple blossoms brimming with love rain your power down from above on me." Allow your candles to burn completely out and keep the flower petals in a circle around the candle until they begin to wilt. Once they have withered, remove them and bury them near your home. Following that, you will discover new love or a new spark in your current relationship.

Chamomile is another excellent herb for rituals involving spellcasting. Simply drinking it has been shown to help alleviate anxiety and promote restful sleep.

Many people also use it to earn money. It has been known to be used to combat hexes that have been cast upon you. When you drink this tea prior to performing a ritual, it can help you focus your energy and heighten it. This herb is frequently used in prosperity and healing spells. You may also find it to be helpful when you use it during dreamwork or trying to remove negative energy from your life. It is frequently used in conjunction with other herbs to amplify its magical properties.

If your life is strewn with negative energies or you have bad feelings around your home, chamomile is great for dealing with it. You will simply start by brewing an extremely strong cup of chamomile tea.

You should then stir a tablespoon of honey into it in a counterclockwise direction. While doing this, you will want to say something like, "Negative energy get out of my way, allow me peace, and all bad feelings go away." From here, you will walk around your house and allow the steam from your hot cup of tea to move around the room. Continue to recite a line like the one from above and focus your intent on removing the negativity from your life or your home.

Mugwort is an extremely versatile herb that almost every witch is going to have available to them at a moment's notice. It is frequently used to Ward off psychic attacks and keep a high level of protection.

Many have found that it is also good when you are working on healing. More often than not, this herb is used to help bring about prophetic dreams. It can also be used in incense for divination. It is important to note that there are a variety of different experiences that are associated with this herb and you need to be careful when working with it.

There are some warnings that you must consider before using this herb. It is not safe for pregnant women to use. It does contain toxins that could build up in the liver if you use it excessively. You should never ingest this herb. Many people are allergic to the pollen that comes off of this plant. Additionally, it has been noted that skin irritation may occur if you come into direct contact with it.

Mugwort is fantastic to use when you are trying to open your psychic channels or if you are working on scrying. To do this, you need to infuse incense with Mugwort essential oil. Once this has been accomplished, burn the incense, and let the smoke and scent fill the room. From here, it is all about intent and meditation. Focus on your desired outcome as the smoke fills the room. The magical properties, scent, and smoke will help put you in the right frame of mind and energise your magical workings.

Last but not least, we are going to discuss the herb Yarrow. It is awesome when you are looking for a protective shield. Additionally, it can help you delve into the spiritual world much more easily. It is commonly used for divination as well as psychic awareness. You will find that when you work with this herb, you can see things more clearly, and your magical experiences are heightened. Yarrow is also good when you are working on healing spells.

A great use for Yarrow in your magical practises is to use it to bring about prophetic dreams. To accomplish this, you will need to create a dream pillow stuffed with the Flowers of the Yarrow plant. You should write your question on a plain white piece of paper and add it to the dream pillow you have created. You will then need to focus your intent. As with all things, this can be done during a deep state of meditation. While you meditate, you should have the dream pillow resting on your lap with your hands on top of it. Focus on your question and push your magical energy and intent into the pillow.

Once this has been accomplished, sleep with only this pillow. The answer to your question should be shown to you during your sleep time that night. If your question is not answered, continue to meditate on your dream pillow daily and sleep on it each night. It should not take long for you to find the answers you are looking for.

While many of the herbs we have talked about have similar magical attributes, it's important that you understand what you're working with before you proceed in using them with spells. They each hold different power and can provide you with different results. This is only a small portion of the huge variety of herbs and spells that are available to you. It is a good place to start. As you continue to grow your skills, you can move on to more intricate spells that use and an even larger variety of herbs.

CHAPTER 6:

HERBAL REMEDIES VS. PRESCRIPTION MEDICATIONS

This section will cover a variety of different herbal remedies.

We're going to look at how herbal remedies can be more beneficial than prescription medications in terms of healing.

Additionally, you will gain valuable insight into the distinctions between the two.

Herbal remedies can be used to aid in the treatment of inflammation, infections, impaired immune function, neurological, and psychological disorders.

Herbs have an incredible number of medicinal applications. It is critical to remember that alternative medicine should never completely replace modern medicine. If you are suffering from a serious illness, it is critical to seek medical attention. Thus, while herbal remedies can be extremely beneficial for a variety of ailments, you should always consider whether or not it is necessary to see a doctor.

Your magical practises and herbs in combination can promote healing on a variety of levels. Herbal medicine is not a new concept. Indeed, it has existed for centuries. There is virtually no point in time when herbal remedies are not being used to aid in the healing process. When combined with your magical practise, the healing potential is exponentially increased.

It is not uncommon for individuals suffering from a variety of ailments to seek the assistance of a herbalist. This is because they are seeking a natural solution. Unfortunately, we live in a society where pills are constantly being pushed at us in order to help us deal with our problems. These pills may cause undesirable side effects. The reason so many people turn to herbal medicines is that they have fewer side effects and produce visible results. Additionally, herbal remedies have been shown to promote more rapid and effective healing.

Additionally, people seek out herbalists due to their distinct demeanour from doctors. Herbalists view us as unique beings.

They deal with our problems on an individual basis. Unfortunately, many physicians view their patients as a source of income. Doctors also have a tendency to view humans uniformly. While we are all composed of the same substances, this does not mean that our ailments should be treated identically every time. Individuals' body chemistry is completely unique, and it is critical to recognise this fact when working on healing. Herbalists understand this and, as a result, will pay attention to the unique characteristics that make you unique rather than lumping you in with everyone else.

Not only are herbal remedies more natural, but they also tend to be much cleaner. Today's medicine contains a wide variety of different chemicals and synthetic materials. These chemicals are corrosive to the human body. Occasionally, they will be able to resolve the issue; however, our bodies are not always capable of doing so. It may leave you feeling worse than when you began due to the possible side effects.

Natural healing was extremely prevalent in ancient times. Herbal remedies were used on a consistent basis. Many people abandoned that belief as modern technology and medical practises convinced them that their way of life was superior. As time has passed, many people have realised that natural healing is one of the more effective methods. Why would we put chemicals into our bodies if we can avoid it?

Numerous herbs are still used in medical sciences today.

This is because the properties of herbal remedies continue to be valuable. Aspirin is an excellent example of this. Its primary component is derived from a shrub. Aspirin will always be derived from the Spiraea plant. This is just one of thousands of herbal remedies that are still used in modern medicine today. Keep in mind, however, that the vast majority of medicine used today is composed of chemicals rather than plant-based ingredients.

Herbal medicine practitioners come in a wide variety of forms.

They all accomplish the same thing, but in distinctive ways.

Herbal medicine can assist you in becoming happier and healthier as a result of the healing properties inherent in the energy that herbs provide. Several herbal practises exist, including Native American herbalism, folkloric herbalism, and many others. Taking the time to investigate each of them can assist you in determining what will fit your beliefs and provide you with the healing you seek.

At this point, we're sure you're aware of the critical role herbs play in both magic and medicine. The energy contained within these enchanted plants can be harnessed to aid in the promotion of healing on both the inside and outside of your body. Whether you are suffering from physical, mental, or spiritual ailments, herbs can assist you in regaining your health.

Herbal Treatments for Common Illnesses

After examining some of the major distinctions between herbal remedies and modern medical practises, we'll examine some specific remedies that you can use in your daily life.

Herbal remedies are available in a variety of forms, making it somewhat difficult to determine which one is best for you. Visiting a herbalist and discussing the type of healing you require is beneficial. They have a thorough understanding of herbs and their medicinal properties.

The first common ailment that we'll examine is inflammation. When our body is injured, one of the initial responses is inflammation. Consider inflammation as a warning signal to our immune system. It alerts our immune system to the need for repair. Inflammation is extremely common, and there are numerous herbs that can be used to treat it without having to take a pill prescribed by your doctor. Let's take a few moments to consider some of the natural ways to manage inflammation.

Frankincense is a resin produced by the Boswellia tree. Ethiopia, Somalia, the Arabian Peninsula, and India are all home to this species. Not only does it alleviate inflammation, but it also aids in the relief of arthritis pain. When combined with Curcumin, also known as Turmeric, it has been shown to be beneficial in the treatment of conditions such as

72

osteoarthritis. If you suffer from chronic inflammation, you can take three to five hundred milligrammes of the extract three times daily.

White Willow Bark: White Willow bark has been used to treat inflammation for a long period of time. It was first observed in use during the Egyptian era. This item has been found to have very similar effects to aspirin. Additionally, it has been noted that white Willow bark has fewer side effects when compared to aspirin. If you suffer from inflammation, you can treat it by consuming 240 milligrammes of white Willow bark extract. Additionally, it can be combined with other herbs to assist with issues such as headaches.

Cat's Claw: Cat's claw is a vine native to Peru. Individuals suffering from bursitis, rheumatoid arthritis, or gastrointestinal disorders may benefit from drinking tea made from the bark of this fine plant. The anti-inflammatory response that our bodies produce can be decreased when this herb is used. Additionally, it aids in maintaining a healthy stomach by protecting you from gastrointestinal inflammation. Making a cat claw T is straightforward. You'll want to use approximately 1,000 milligrammes of this vine's bark. Eight ounces of hot water should be added. It's also worth noting that you can purchase cats claw as a dried extract.

Typically, you'll want to consume between forty and sixty milligrammes daily to combat inflammation.

It is critical to note that these are just a few of the numerous herbs that are beneficial for reducing inflammation

Natural relief is truly possible for a variety of inflammatory conditions. Consult a herbalist or discuss additional natural remedies with your doctor before making medical decisions.

After discussing inflammation, we'll move on to another common ailment. Each of us will contract an infection at some point in our lives. Typically, when we have an infection, an antibiotic such as amoxicillin or penicillin is prescribed. This has aided a large number of people in overcoming infectious diseases for an extended period of time. While these practises are highly effective, there are some natural remedies that can aid in the healing process. Natural antibiotics have far fewer adverse effects than prescription antibiotics. As we did previously, let's examine several different natural remedies that can assist your body in fighting an infection.

Echinacea: Echinacea is used by traditional healers and Native American healers to aid in the healing of infected wounds. Additionally, it aids in the treatment of infections such as toxic shock syndrome and strep throat. The extract from this plant is effective against a wide variety of bacteria. Additionally, it has been discovered to aid in the fight against the inflammation caused by bacteria during infection. The amount you take will depend on how you consume this item. Many people find success when they use it in the form of tea. Six to eight ounces of echinacea tea four times daily is sufficient for the majority of people. You should begin drinking it immediately upon noticing any signs of infection. You will most likely need to consume it over a ten-day period.

Goldenseal: This herb's root is frequently dried and used to make a variety of different medications. It is quite effective at treating urinary tract infections. Additionally, it can aid in the treatment of bacterial diarrhoea. The majority of the time, it is consumed in a T or swallowed in a capsule. Capsules are typically less effective. Tea is rapidly absorbed by our bodies. Recently, it was discovered that goldenseal can be used to aid in the treatment of skin infections. It is critical to note that this herb may interact with other prescription medications, so it is critical to consult your doctor before beginning. It contains a number of components found in natural antibiotics. It is not, however, safe to take by pregnant women or infants.

There are a few additional herbs that can aid in the fight against infection. However, these are the two that are most frequently used.

The data on the other herbs is not as reliable as the data on these two. Because an infection can be quite serious, it is critical to consult with your herbalist or physician to ensure that you are using the correct herb to treat your condition.

Maintaining a healthy immune system is always a good idea. A strong immune system can help you avoid becoming ill as frequently. Your body will be better equipped to deal with illnesses such as the common cold or the flu. The stronger your immune system, the healthier you are in general. When it comes to living a healthy lifestyle, having a strong immune system is critical. You will undoubtedly be surprised to learn that there are a variety of herbs that can assist in boosting your immune system. Consider a few of them.

Oregano: Oregano is an excellent herb to incorporate into your routine when trying to strengthen your immune system. It contains a variety of vital vitamins that you may be deficient in. Vitamin C, a comma OK, and vitamin E are examples of these. Each of these vitamins has been demonstrated to benefit the immune system. Additionally, oregano is anti-inflammatory and beneficial against fungal infections. Oregano oils have been shown in studies to aid the body's fight against MRSA and listeria. When using oregano oil, it is necessary to be aware of possible side effects. Certain individuals are allergic to it. If you have a basil, mint, sage, or lavender allergy, you should probably avoid this herb. Pregnant or nursing women should also avoid oregano oil. It is not approved for use in children, and you should absolutely consult your doctor if you have any type of bleeding disorder. It can be prepared as a tincture, or many people prefer to take it as capsules. If capsules are used, three 150-milligram doses per day will suffice.

Licorice Root: Licorice root has a slightly different action. It is beneficial for a variety of different conditions. These herbs work because they stimulate your adrenal glands. Additionally, it aids in managing your stress responses. Our immune systems are inextricably linked to our adrenal glands. When our bodies are stressed, the adrenal glands and immune systems are depleted. This can expose you to attacks that your immune system is unable to defend against. Thus, by promoting the health of your adrenal glands, you are also promoting the health of your immune system. The best way to use this herb to boost your immune system is to make a tea from it. The plant's leaves can be crushed and used to create it. Consume no more than six to eight ounces of licorice-flavored tea per day. This small amount can significantly benefit your adrenal glands and, consequently, your immune system.

Turmeric: Turmeric is a superfood. It strengthens the immune system and is loaded with antioxidants. It can aid in the treatment of inflammation, viruses, and a variety of fungal infections. Numerous people report that it significantly aids in the treatment of the common cold. Additionally, it can aid in the treatment of more serious conditions such as cancer or the flu. This herb is extremely versatile and can benefit anyone who wishes to live a healthier lifestyle. It is extremely popular to consume this herb as a tea. This type of tea does not require a large serving to boost your immune system. A single eight-ounce glass per day should suffice. When dealing with more serious problems, you should consult a herbalist to determine the proper dosage.

Obviously, maintaining a strong immune system will benefit your overall health. When your immune system is strong, combating bacteria, inflammation, infection, and other issues becomes easier. You will recover faster and resume your normal life. Bear in mind that we've only touched on a few of the numerous herbs that can be used to assist in boosting and supporting your immune system.

Additionally, you can enhance your neurological function or brain power through the use of herbs and herbal remedies. Indeed, it is surprising to learn, but the effects of herbs on conditions such as Alzheimer's can be quite dramatic. When we begin to incorporate various herbs into our diets, our overall cognition improves. Let's take a look at a variety of herbs that can help you improve your neural function.

Sage: Sage is a very common herb that the majority of people use in their cooking. It has an extremely pungent odour. It has been shown to be effective in reversing the effects of Alzheimer's disease. It contains a variety of compounds that aid in the improvement of neurological functions. You do not need to take any special precautions when consuming this herb. It can be used in a wide variety of different food preparations. This category includes items such as tomato sauce and chicken. Additionally, there is no precise measurement for the amount of sage required to improve mental functions. Consuming it on a daily basis will demonstrate reward in your cognition levels.

Turmeric: Turmeric is also an excellent way to improve your brain's health. It has a variety of beneficial effects. It aids in the removal of protein fragments from the brain, slowing the progression of Alzheimer's disease. Additionally, it assists in preventing the breakdown of the nerves in your brain. Turmeric is another versatile ingredient that can be incorporated into a wide variety of recipes. Although the daily dose is not precise, eating it frequently and including it in your diet can help ensure that your brain remains extremely healthy and alert.

Ginkgo-Biloba: Ginkgo-Biloba is a supplement that is used to treat dementia and other cognitive problems. It has been used in this capacity for an unusually long period of time. It is well-known for its ability to increase circulation and blood flow to the brain. Several of the results of testing are inconclusive. However, those who consume this herb on a daily basis report improved cognitive function. Additionally, it has been suggested that it aids in the decline of Alzheimer's Disease.

Lemon Balm: Lemon balm tea has been used for centuries to help alleviate anxiety and insomnia symptoms. It has recently been discovered that it can also help with height and cognitive function. This tea should be consumed on a more frequent basis and for a longer duration than many other medications. The majority consume it on a daily basis for at least four months. There is no risk associated with drinking this tea daily, or even twice daily, for an extended period of time. This reduces the effects of Alzheimer's disease and dementia. The improvement in cognitive function is quite remarkable.

Combating dementia and Alzheimer's disease can be extremely difficult. These two conditions impose a significant burden on not only the person who is afflicted but also on those who care about them. It is remarkable to be able to improve cognitive function when one of these two conditions exists. There are numerous other herbs that can benefit individuals who do not have one of these conditions but wish to improve their neurological function. There are numerous books and articles that can be used to obtain this information. Additionally, you can consult a herbalist or your physician to discuss various herbal remedies that can help boost your neurological functions.

Doctors are quick to prescribe antidepressants to patients with mental health problems. These are associated with a slew of negative side effects. They can make you feel as if you're living in a perpetual fog or as if you're uninterested in anything. This is a significant reason why many people turn to herbal remedies to assist them in overcoming mental or psychological issues. There are numerous herbs with research to support their ability to alleviate the symptoms of mental illness. They have a wide range of applications, including baths, tinctures, cooking, and salves. This article will discuss a variety of different herbs that can be used to help alleviate the symptoms of mental illness.

Saffron: Saffron is frequently used as an expectorant, sedative, pain reliever, and antidepressant.

Not only is it beneficial for treating depression, but it can also help your nervous system maintain a state of calmness. Its effects will help you feel less anxious. Saffron is significantly more effective than antidepressants such as Fluoxetine. It aids in the relaxation of our muscles, which in turn aids in the relaxation of the mind. Surprisingly, it also aids in digestion and increases appetite. This is critical because many people who suffer from depression consume far fewer calories than their bodies require.

Licorice: If you're looking for a natural antidepressant, antiviral, expectorant, or anti-inflammatory, licorice may be beneficial. Licorice contains compounds that stimulate our adrenal glands. Our stress levels have a significant effect on our adrenal functions. As a result, when our adrenal glands are functioning optimally, we experience a decrease in depression, stress, and anxiety.

Numerous mental illnesses are caused by problems with our nervous system. Thus, by incorporating licorice into your routine, you can assist in combating the negative symptoms associated with mental health issues.

Bacopa: Bacopa is still widely used today as it was centuries ago due to its efficacy as an antidepressant. Additionally, it improves a person's focus and energy levels. It contributes by reducing stress levels. Additionally, it enables our bodies to respond more positively to the stress we encounter on a daily basis. Bacopa contains compounds that enhance our brain's functionality. This is especially true when it comes to our cognitive ability and memory. Many people use this herb on a daily basis to treat anxiety. It has been shown to be effective in the treatment of post-traumatic stress disorder. Consuming Bacopa is also beneficial for those who suffer from memory loss, learning difficulties, and difficulty focusing.

Mental illness is not to be taken lightly. As is always the case, consulting a herbalist or your physician prior to attempting to create a regimen of herbal supplements to help with your ailments is the best course of action. Numerous items on our list have proven to be successful, and there are several others that are equally successful. Bear in mind that we are all slightly different, and thus what works for one person may not work as well for another.

Herbal & Magical Remedies

Each of these remedies is quite effective on its own. It is not necessary to use magic to discover the power of herbs. However, if you want to boost the healing power of herbal remedies, incorporating magic into the mix will work quite well for you. By connecting with the energy that surrounds us, we can speed up the healing process.

Adding magic to your herbal remedies is not difficult. Generally, all that is required is for you to meditate on the ingredients of the remedy you are about to use. By channelling your intention and energy into the items, they will be able to facilitate the healing process.

Including a mantra in your meditation practise when enhancing the effectiveness of a herbal remedy is always a good idea. There are numerous different mantras, and which one you use will depend on the type of healing you are attempting to perform.

For generations, herbal remedies and magical practises have coexisted. All of your healing spells will almost certainly include some form of herb. Thus, it's easy to see how incorporating magic into your remedies would be just as effective. From the beginning of the process of creating a herbal remedy, you should incorporate positive energy and intent into each step. This will equip your healing efforts with everything they require to succeed.

CHAPTER 7:

ENHANCING HERBAL SPELLS

Clearly, herbs possess considerable power on their own. However, there are a variety of different tools that you can use to augment the power of your spells. This chapter will examine how candles, crystals, stones, gems, and meditation can truly enhance the power of any spell you are attempting to cast.

We'll begin by examining the power of candles. Candles are used in almost every magic ritual and spell.

They come in a variety of colours, and each colour enhances your power in a different area. Candles are used in almost every culture and religion that exists today.

Candles

When you examine the history of candles in relation to magic, you will discover that they are considered sacred. They aided in our ascension out of the darkness with their fire. Additionally, candles are associated with the deceased.

There are candle-based spells that enable you to communicate with those in the afterlife, locate treasure, and enhance your dream states.

The precise date at which candles began to be used in magical practises is unknown. Their use dates all the way back to the time of the ancient Egyptians. Additionally, they have been used in virtually every culture and religion since the dawn of mankind.

Candle flames were regarded as enigmatic. Individuals discovered that by gazing into the flame and entering a meditative state, they could access higher states of consciousness. Some claimed to be able to communicate with higher beings, while others claimed to be able to see into the future.

Candle-based magical rituals are extremely common. They are used to aid in the manifestation of love spells, prophetic dreams, insight, enlightenment, and removing hexes, among other things. Candles are an integral part of the magic.

Pagans have always used and will continue to use candles in their rituals. They are frequently placed on altars or at the intersections of a cast circle's quadrants.

They are frequently used at the pentagram's points.

The colour of a candle has a variety of effects on a spell. Colors have their own vibrations and properties that must be considered if they are to be used to energise a herbal spell. The majority of people anoint their candles prior to casting a spell. This is accomplished through the use of various oils. The type of oil that you use will depend on the type of spell that you are casting. To anoint your candle, simply rub oil into it and focus on the spell's intention.

Take a moment to consider the various colours of candles available. Additionally, we'll discuss the types of spells for which each colour is best suited. Due to the vibration of coloured candles, they enhance magical work.

When someone is casting a spell for strength, white candles are frequently used. They are also excellent for spells that seek spiritual truths. Purification or purity spells will also benefit from the use of a white candle. Many people discover that by burning white candles during the process, they can reach deeper levels of meditation. Additionally, you can use white candles to break curses and attract positive forces into your life.

Pink candles should be used when casting friendship or love spells. Pink candles are ideal for achieving a state of harmony in your life. They can also be used to instil a sense of calm in your home.

When attempting to improve one's physical health or strength, red candles should be used. Additionally, red is the colour associated with sexuality and passion. Therefore, if you're looking for a boost in your romantic life, a red candle may be beneficial. Additionally, some people use red candles in protection spells.

Orange candles can assist in providing you with courage. They assist you when casting communication spells. When attempting to improve one's concentration, casting spells with orange candles is beneficial. Additionally, they are fantastic when attempting to solve problems that appeared to have no solution. Orange candles can also be beneficial when casting spells for one's own or another's encouragement.

Yellow candles can be beneficial when casting persuasion spells. They contribute to the spellcaster's increased charm and confidence. If you're looking to boost your memory or study skills, an orange candle can be extremely beneficial.

Green is the colour associated with prosperity and wealth. Thus, using green candles during one of these two types of spells will be extremely beneficial.

Green candles are also beneficial when performing a healing ritual on someone. Additionally, you can use them when casting fertility spells. Green is also an excellent colour for spells aimed at improving one's luck.

Blue candles are extremely adaptable. They are ideal for use in spiritual or psychic awareness spells. Additionally, they are used when casting spells for protection while sleeping and daily peace. Prophetic dreams can also come true when blue candle spells are cast.

Purple candles have a plethora of magical applications. If you lack ambition, incorporating a purple candle into your spells can assist you in obtaining it. Additionally, they are effective at reversing any curses placed on you or your loved ones. Purple candles are excellent for speeding up the healing process. Additionally, it can be used to assist you in establishing authority among a group of peers. If you're looking for an extra boost to any type of spell, a purple candle is always a good choice.

While gold candles are not as versatile as white candles, they are quite powerful.

They are ideal for casting protection spells.

Additionally, if you're seeking enlightenment and a connection to the universe or higher powers, incorporating a gold candle into your spells or meditation practises will increase the strength and ease with which you achieve your desired outcome.

Silver candles, like gold candles, are not particularly versatile.

They can be incorporated into spells to aid in the development of a person's intuition. Additionally, they can assist in eliciting information from your subconscious mind.

Finally, but certainly not least, let us discuss black candles. They can be incorporated into spells to help mitigate the impact of a loved one's death. They can also be used to alleviate someone's sadness or discord. Black handles are excellent for dealing with negativity or negative energy in your life or home.

As you can see, candles play a fairly significant role in the art of spellcasting. When you incorporate candles into your herbal magic routines, the potency of those spells is significantly increased. This will ensure that you are able to manifest the desired outcome. It is critical to use the correct coloured candle and to light it for the appropriate amount of time. Herbal spells combined with candle magic will produce amazing results.

Crystals, Stones, and Gems

From the time of the ancient Sumerians, crystals, stones, and gems \shave then regarded highly. They were found to enhance the power of spells. Regardless if you were trying to improve your health, game protection, or rid evil spirits from your life's crystals, stones, and gems can help in achieving your desired outcome. This was true way back in the day, and it continues to be true today.

Ancient Greek cultures also found that they could harness the power of crystals, stones, and gems. In fact, a lot of the words we use to name these items come from the Greek. These are only a couple of examples of where crystals, stones, and gems have played a role.

Basically, every religion or culture has information in regard to the power of these three items.

There was a period of time that these important tools were pushed out of sight. It was thought that their power was that of superstition.

As time moved on, experiments we're done to see if crystals, gems, \sand stones had any effects at all. It was surprising to find that they affected people on a physical, mental, and emotional level.

This helped to rekindle the use of crystals, stones, and gems in magical practises. Old traditions were combined with these newfound ideas, and the popularity of these items soared. Today there are many books, articles, and other works that provide \teachings toward the power of using crystals in your everyday life.

Crystal therapy and magic can be used to solve a variety of different problems.

It is important to note that there are some differences between crystals, stones, and gems. It is not always simple to figure out what you are looking at, so knowing these differences is important when you are trying to work on a spell. Gems are made from minerals.

They are typically very rare. Gyms are pulled from the earth. From there, they are, typically, cut, and polished. Jewelry and other forms of decoration typically involve gemstones. The nature of them can be precious or semi-precious. Diamonds, emeralds, and sapphires are all examples of precious gems.

Regular stones and gemstones are different things. Standard stones \swill hold some power, but they're not going to be as attractive looking as gemstones. They do not have as much value monetarily nor do they hold the same kind of power that gemstones will. Regular stones can be found in nature, and their power can be utilised right away.

There are an enormous variety of crystals, stones, and gems available to you. We could not possibly go through each and every one. However, we'll examine some of the most powerful and versatile options available. They can assist in giving your spells the extra oomph they require to achieve true manifestation.

Amethyst is the first crystal we'd like to discuss. It possesses considerable authority. You will discover how spiritual this crystal is. When your life is lacking in peace or stability, incorporating an amethyst into your spells will assist you in overcoming these obstacles. Additionally, it is an excellent crystal for casting powerful spells. It can provide you with increased energy levels during meditation, ensuring that your focus remains focused. Additionally, it aids in the promotion of calmness, which puts you in the proper frame of mind for meditation.

Agate is a fairly common stone. It's fantastic when you're casting spells of strength. It will assist you in discovering your mind, body, and spirit's strength. Many people use it when casting courage spells. Additionally, it is beneficial when attempting to regain control of your emotions.

Because heightened emotions can make it difficult to see the truth of a situation, casting a spell with agate for a clear mind will enable you to see what is truly happening and accept those truths.

Blue quartz can be used to amplify purification spells. It makes no difference whether the purification is mental, emotional, or physical. This crystal is extremely calming and can assist you in finding the words necessary to communicate effectively with others.

Additionally, clear calcite possesses a plethora of magical properties. Calcite comes in a variety of colours. Clear calcite will assist you in attaining higher states of consciousness and spiritual development. Golden calcite can be used for relaxation spells and to assist you in reaching different realms.

Fire agate is a stone that many people use in courage spells. Additionally, it is extremely potent when used in protection spells. If you need to adjust the negative thought patterns you've been experiencing recently, meditating with this stone can assist you in doing so. Due to the incredible connection this stone has with the earth, grounding spells benefit when fire agate is present.

This stone's energy is very calming and gives people a sense of security.

If your life appears to be out of balance, casting spells with green Jade may be beneficial. This common yet potent stone has the ability to bring tranquillity to the tumultuous nature of life. Additionally, it can help you achieve mental, physical, and spiritual clarity. Additionally, it can be used in spells to attract love into your life. Many discover that it also works well when casting spells for increased courage or wisdom.

Labradorite is a less common but extremely powerful stone. If you are attempting to work on your chakra system, this can assist you in more easily directing energies. It can help you achieve greater balance more quickly, which will benefit every aspect of your life. Your physical and spiritual selves will become more connected. This stone can assist you in establishing a connection with the universe or higher powers through spellcasting.

Moonstone can assist us in establishing new beginnings. Moonstone is advantageous when performing any type of lunar magic. If you're looking for increased intuition or are struggling with life changes, casting spells aided by the power of moonstone can assist you in resolving these issues. Numerous people discover that simply having this stone in their possession helps to lift their spirits. Additionally, it has the ability to enhance psychic abilities and assist you in connecting with your subtle body. Moonstone can also be quite beneficial when working on astral projection and lucid dreaming projects.

As with candles, stones can greatly enhance the power of your herbal rituals and spells. When crystals, stones, or gems are added to magical workings, you are enhancing their energy, which can be quite amazing. This is especially true for herbal magic, as all of these items originate from the earth. Their lines of authority are entwined.

Acquainting yourself with and amassing a collection of crystals, gems, and stones will assist you in manifesting a variety of different spells. Whether you're seeking love, peace, prosperity, money, or other desires, combining herbal spells with crystals, stones, and gems will assist in bringing them to fruition.

Crystals are a bit different from gemstones and stones. They're always in the form of a pattern. This is how they naturally occur.

They are geometric in shape. The angles of the crystal are all in symmetry. Crystals are three dimensional. And the order of them is easily seen this way. You should keep in mind that crystals cannot be gems, but gems can be crystals.

Of the three categories, gemstones are the most expensive. Crystals are somewhere in between common stones and gemstones when it comes to price. This is why many people prefer to work with crystals as they fit into their budgets more easily. You can find crystals in many decorative pieces including jewellery, ambulance, and vases.

When you need an extra boost of energy when casting a spell, crystals are a fantastic go-to option.

Meditation

Throughout this book, we have discussed meditation at length. That is because it is such a critical component of spellcasting.

If it is not already, meditation should become a daily practise. The power that meditation enables you to develop is absolutely incredible.

When you meditate, your mind relaxes and you gain the ability to shift your focus away from what is directly in front of you and toward the world around you. As you begin to do this, you will notice that you can manipulate the energies around you. Additionally, frequent meditation will help you gain greater clarity and insight into yourself and those around you.

Many people find time throughout the day to meditate. It is possible to do so for a variety of different reasons. When their day is less than ideal, some people meditate to regain their composure or peace. Others use it to rebalance themselves when they become unbalanced.

Clearly, meditation is a significant component of magical practises and should be performed at nearly every stage of spellcasting.

All of your herbs and herbal spells require some time for meditation. This will assist you in conveying your intent to them. When the tools used in magical rituals and spells are imbued with intent, manifestation becomes much easier. These herbs will absorb your intention and then channel their power to bring it to fruition.

Certain individuals have difficulty entering a meditative state. Others come easily and naturally. As with anything, if you initially struggle with meditation, all you need to do is be patient and continue practising. Today, you can choose from a wide variety of guided meditations. Guided meditation can significantly ease the process of getting your mind in the right zone.

Meditation is an ancient practise that dates all the way back to the beginning of time. It is a practise that will endure for future generations.

This is because true enlightenment and comprehension of the world require a serene mind, body, and soul. When we meditate regularly, attaining this state of calmness becomes significantly easier.

CHAPTER 8:

MOON MAGIC

We're going to cover a good deal of information about full moon magic in the final chapter of this book. The moon is involved in every aspect of life on Earth. Moon phases are determined by three bodies. The sun, the earth, and the moon are the three.

The moon, like our lives, follows a cycle. We can literally feel the moon phases' push and pull. This astrological body is the closest to the earth of all. It does, in fact, exert considerable influence over our emotions. Additionally, it has an effect on the earth, including the tides.

As most people are aware, the moon undergoes various lunar phases. It progresses from new to full moon. There are eight distinct moon phases. The moon is always the same; however, how it appears to us on earth changes due to the sun's light reflection.

The position of the sun and moon determines what we see in the Night Sky. A lunar cycle lasts slightly less than 30 days.

Each lunar phase has a unique set of characteristics. A new moon is also known as a waxing moon. It is the first full moon of the lunar cycle. When the moon and the sun align and there is no trace of the moon visible at night, this is referred to as a new moon. When attempting a new beginning or adopting a new mindset, it is advantageous to cast spells during the new moon. The possibilities are virtually limitless. Additionally, the new moon is an excellent time for releasing fear and setting intentions. Attempting to manifest desires and connecting with higher powers is best done during the new moon.

We enter the phase of the waxing crescent immediately following the new moon. It is slightly brighter, and is the precursor to the full moon. It assists us in committing to the intentions we set at the new moon. During this lunar phase, you must remain steadfast in your intentions. It can be a time when people revert to old patterns if they do not remain focused on the desired outcomes. There are not many magical spells performed during this moon phase.

We begin with a waxing Crescent and progress to the first quarter moon. This is the phase of the moon when it is halfway full. At this stage of the moon, our future plans will begin to take shape. You may need to recast or meditate on new moon spells to ensure they have the energy necessary to manifest. Throughout the spell casting process, an effort must be made. At this stage of the lunar cycle, you may cast spells to invoke new visions of your future.

Following the waxing crescent is the waxing gibbous. When the moon is nearly full, its energy is amplified. If you need to alter your spell work in any way, now is the time to do so. Many people find this lunar phase to be stressful. Spells are preparing to manifest, which can add anxiety to one's life. The best course of action is to maintain focus and to continue meditating on your desired outcome. During this phase of the moon, you may need to continuously bring energy into your home and interior life, as exhaustion is a possibility.

Now we enter the full moon phase. This is the point at which we can see the entire number. Any spells cast during the new moon phase will be fulfilled or manifest. Our intentions should have been sustained throughout the lunar cycle, so that we can see the fruits of our labours as we enter the phase of the new moon. Our spells frequently come to fruition during this time of the month. When your spells come to fruition, it is critical that you express gratitude to the universe for assisting you in accomplishing your goals.

The waning gibbous moon occurs after the full moon. This phase serves as a reminder that we must share our findings and efforts with the rest of the world. Consider how your manifestations benefit the world around you. Meditation during this moon phase is critical because it can help you gain a better understanding of your accomplishments and establish a sense of self-worth. Make a point of expressing gratitude to the universe's higher powers during this moon cycle.

When the moon reaches its final quarter phase, it is referred to as a waning half-moon.

This time around. Will allow for the expansion of our consciousness. It will allow us to take a good look at what we have accomplished. For some, this is a time of crisis, as the end of a lunar cycle approaches. Final outcomes are difficult to alter, even more so after the manifestation of previously cast spells. If you're looking for a way to see the bigger picture in life, this is the moon cycle to do so. Almost always, prophecies and visions are born during this time of the month.

The final phase of the moon is referred to as the waning Crescent. This is the end of the cycle, and the time has come for you to purge your life of any negativity that has crept in. You're about to enter the new moon phase and the stage of new beginnings. Many people discover that receiving messages from spirits and higher powers is significantly easier at this point due to the much thinner veil between realities.

The majority of people prefer to work with magic at the new or full moon. Keep in mind that it is frequently preferable to cast your spells and intentions during the new moon in order for them to manifest with the full moon's energy. While some practitioners work with moon magic throughout the phases, it is most common to cast spells or perform rituals on the new or full moon.

By the power of the moon, you can work through any magical spells, but some will work better than others. Moon magic also aids in the opening of our memories and rerouting us to what is truly important. It establishes a link between us and our emotions, as well as with the universe's higher powers. It can assist us in better understanding how to care for ourselves and others.

All spells, regardless of whether they are cast with crystals, stones, gems, candles, or herbs, can be cast during the lunar phases. Some of these items are inextricably linked to the moon, making them more potent tools for casting spells during a new or full moon.

The son is associated with stones, crystals, gems, candles, and herbs. Obviously, casting these spells with sun-related items at night will not work as well.

Now that we've discussed a variety of facts about the moon's phases, let's move on. There are numerous activities that you can undertake during the full moon phase. Consider several different spells that will easily manifest when cast during a full moon.

If you've been having financial difficulties, attracting money into your life is as simple as casting money spells during the full moon. The full moon's energy is at its peak. This has the potential to amp up wealth or financial spells. Many people achieve their greatest success with financial gain spells when they perform them during this phase of the moon. This is because energy levels are abundant, allowing you to focus your intention and supercharge the energy that flows through you and your magical tools.

The majority of people find a full moon extremely romantic. As a result, it is an excellent time to cast love spells. If you are experiencing emotional turmoil, the full moon is the optimal time to cast spells to alleviate it. Love spells cast during the full moon can help us become more receptive to romantic love and to all that life has to offer. By incorporating candles, herbs, and crystals into your love spells or charms, you can amp up their effectiveness. Concentrate on your affirmations or mantras to attract the love you've been seeking.

Additionally, the full moon is an excellent time to charge your tools. Allowing your crystals, stones, or gems to be bathed in the light of the full moon can infuse them with an enormous amount of energy. When you use these crystals, stones, or gems to cast spells, their enhanced power will be immediately noticeable. Manifestation will also become easier once your crystals have been empowered by the moon's energy.

If you've noticed negative energies in your home, it's beneficial to clear them during the full moon. The surrounding magical energies are ideal for casting blessings or protection spells in your space. Clearly, setting an intention is critical for removing any unwanted or negative energy that may linger around you or your home.

Many people discover that the most accurate tarot card readings occur during the full moon. If you're looking for a glimpse into the future, reading your tarot during the full moon is beneficial.

The moon's power aids in providing insight into future prophecies. You are not required to be able to read your own tarot cards. Finding a reputable tarot card reader during the full moon can provide invaluable insight into the direction your life is taking.

The full moon provides the most light we will ever receive during the darkest hours of the year. If you're looking for clarity in a difficult situation or want to shed light on a subject, casting insight spells during the full moon will yield the best results. Many people prefer to cast divination spells during this time period because true insight can be found in the full moon's light. During the full moon, your magical power will be amplified, and as a result, your intentions will manifest more easily.

We have all encountered difficulties in our daily lives. They can be observed in relation to health, relationships, and work. If you need to cast spells to cleanse your life of negativity, the full moon is the best time to do so. Many people perform banishing rituals during the full moon because it can provide the necessary power for these spells to work. There are several very simple spells that can be performed. Consider one.

A simple ritual for banishing would be to jot down whatever it is in your life that is weighing you down on a blank piece of white paper. Roll the piece of paper away from you in a small scroll-like fashion.

Wax or a small piece of twine can be used to seal it. From here, you'll transfer it to a jar and cover it with sea salt. It is critical to note that you should completely fill the jar. Top the salt with a feather that was found in nature and then seal the jar. You must keep this jar for three moon cycles before burying the salt and feather in the earth and burning the scroll. After you've burned the scroll, you'll notice that the burdens that were contained within begin to lift from your spirit.

As is the case with everything, this is only a sampling of the numerous types of spells and rituals that can be performed during the full moon. The possibilities are truly limitless. Full moon magic has the potential to be extremely potent. Always begin with the fundamentals before attempting more difficult spells or rituals, as the results may not be what you intended.

From the time we are small children, we are all aware of the full moon's power. It has a profound effect on us. The power that magical practises impart is truly astounding. If you've never worked with full moon magic before, you're going to be pleasantly surprised by how it feels as you work through your spellcasting practise. During the full moon, group spellcasting is also quite effective. Working with the full moon becomes even more amazing as you progress to intermediate or advanced level spells. This requires time, effort, study, practise, and study. However, once you invest in education, you will be amazed at what you can manifest during the full moon.

CONCLUSION

We appreciate your perseverance in reading all the way to the end of Wicca Herbal Magic; we hope it was informative and equipped you with the tools necessary to accomplish your goals, whatever they may be.

The next step is to begin cultivating, collecting, and storing a diverse array of magical herbs. To get started, you can purchase some from a local market or greenhouse. Naturally, growing your own herbs for magical purposes is always the most advantageous method. From the moment they are planted, you will be able to provide them with positive energy and intent.

Herbalism is not difficult, but it does require practise. With patience and time, you can gain a thorough understanding of a variety of herbs and their magical properties. With this knowledge, you will be able to confidently participate in Wiccan rituals, spells, magical baths, and other Wiccan practises.

Herbs are excellent for both spellcasting and healing. Numerous ailments can be easily treated with herbs, which allows you to avoid the harmful chemicals found in pharmaceuticals. This can result in a more contented and healthy life. While there is a time and place for more modern medications, natural remedies are always a better option. Remember to seek guidance from a herbalist or your physician prior to attempting to heal yourself or others with herbal remedies.

Utilizing crystals, stones, gems, and candles can significantly increase the potency of your spells. Remember to take your time with spellcasting endeavours; haste never served anyone well. Continue practising and concentrating, and you will quickly recognise the power of herbal magic.